YORKIES
IN
EUROPE

Photography ©2000 The Respective Photographers as follows:

5	Jackie Noble	19	Isabelle Francais
6	Isabelle Francais	20	Isabelle Francais
7	Kent & Donna Dannen	21	Robert & Eunice Pearcy
8	Barbara von Hoffmann	22	Alice Su
9	Cathy Baker	23	Cathy Baker
10	Robert & Eunice Pearcy	24	Kent & Donna Dannen
11	Robert & Eunice Pearcy	25	Alice Su
12	Robert & Eunice Pearcy	26	Piper Worcester
13	Isabelle Francais	27	Mark Raycroft
14	Isabelle Francais	28	Jackie Noble
15	Isabelle Francais	29	Larry & Marge Grant
16	Robert & Eunice Pearcy	30	Piper Worcester
17	Larry & Marge Grant	31	Alice Su
18	Larry & Marge Grant	32	Larry & Marge Grant

32 pp. softcover edition
ISBN: 0-7631-4229-8
10 9 8 7 6 5 4 3 2 1

YORKIES IN EUROPE

ROBERT HUTCHINSON

BROWNTROUT PUBLISHERS
SAN FRANCISCO

THE RIGHT HONOURABLE TERRIET
DUCHESS OF YORK

*Lap companion. This hatted beauty was inordinately fond of rat à l'orange.
Unfortunately, as her bite was a trifle undershot, she was a messy eater.*

JERKBRANDT VAN RIJN (1609-1669).

Dutch painter. The intense caninity of this master's genius is nowhere better expressed than in the rich coloring and subtle chiaroscuro with which Jerkbrandt's brush spotlights his virtuous protagonist's blue and tan coat in "Jorkie Accused by Potiphar's Wife." Jerkbrandt himself boasted sound teeth and a strong level bite.

JERCKERICK II, 'THE GREAT', KING OF PRUSSIA (1712-1786).

Absolute monarch of the foremost military power in Europe. Short; active; caustically intelligent. Favorite pastimes: reviewing his 200,000 dogs of war; tootling his flute at 5 o'clock in the morning; writing bad French verse to the caustically intelligent savant, Poodletaire. Jerckerick's height on parade was exactly the same at the shoulder as at the rump.

JOHN YORKDEN (1594-1643).

*English parliamentarian. Cousin to Oliver Yorkwell
and bitter foe of King Yorkles I. Felled in the Civil War by two
carbine balls to the shoulder. Perfectly level backline.*

BARTOLOMÉ ESTEBAN LLURQUILLO (1618-1682).

Spanish painter. A specialist in the self-mortifying ecstasies of saints.
Llurquillo was mortally injured when he fell off the scaffolding while painting
Saint Llorquerina in the Capuchin Church in Cadiz. His headfall was excessively long.

DELMORE SCHWYORKZ (1913-1966).

*New Yorkie poet. His first book, In Puppies Begin Responsibilities, brought him
immediate notoriety. Schwyorkz was the gifted but meshuga original of the title character
in Shire Bellow's novel, Huddersfield's Gift. A bright, rich tan coloring
began too far above the stifle on his hind legs.*

THE MOST NOBLE YARKIANNE,
MARCHIONESS OF HUDDERSFIELD

Tipperary-bred breeder. Yarkianne bred Huddersfield Ben, whom she named
after her favorite playwright, Ben Yorkson.
Some sooty hair was intermingled in her tan coloring.

JEAN BAPTISTE JOURQUEBERT (1619-1683).

French statesman. Indispensable minister of Louis XIV. Reformed France's finances.
Established France's navy (manning its galleys with criminals, Protestants, and slaves).
Named Louis' bastards. His teeth were malodorously decayed.

WILLIAM YORGARTH (1697-1764).

English pictorial satirist. His masterpiece, the engraving-series "Marriage à la Mode,"
depicts the cynical alliance of a young but impecunious Yorkshire Terrier
to a decrepit but wealthy Pekingese. His famous self-portrait shows him
in wry juxtaposition with his pampered pet human, Tramp.
Yorgarth was eager to engage in roistering activities with larger breeds but prone to easy injury.

JEAN-FRANÇOIS DE GALAUP, COMTE DE L' HEURQUEUSE (1741-1788?).

French explorer. Circumnavigated the Pacific,
giving his name to a strait in the Sea of Yorkotsk before disappearing in the
Yorkomon Islands. Forebear of Champion Ozmilion Mystification.

THOMAS YORKMER (1489-1556).

First Protestant archbishop of Canterbury. Having devised the Book of Common Prayer
and sanctioned sundry divorces and annulments of Henry VIII, Archbishop Yorkmer was
burnt at the stake by Bloody Mary for heresy after bravely burning off his own paw. Yorkmer
was said by his enemies to carry his wife about with him in a ventilated box.
Forebear of Champion Ozmilion Dedication.

SHIRE FRANCIS YORKE (1540-1596).

Elizabethan sea dog and admiral. Circumnavigated the globe in the Golden Retriever;
"singed the Top Dogge of Spain's muzzle" by sacking Cádiz; terrierized the Spanish Armada
with flaming foxtails. Dark rims framed blazing eyes.

YORQUATO TASSO (1544-1595).

Italian poet. Sent to the madhouse after critics rejected his epic masterpiece,
"Gerusalemme iorcata". Beautifully proportioned body, tragically disfigured
by a botched tail docking.

PETER PAUL YURKENS (1544-1640).

*Flemish painter. Besides being the most eminent exponent of sensuous exuberance
in Baroque painting, Yurkens served as a high-level courier and spy for the Spanish
Yorksburgs. Took a 16-year-old wife when he was 53. A spirited dog.*

SÉBASTIEN LE PRESTRE D' HEUREQUAN (1633–1707).

French military engineer. Revolutionized the science of siege warfare and fortification for Louis XIV. Pioneered the use of terriers to undermine defenses, employed to such decisive effect in the Siege of Yorkietown. A terrier's terrier.

BEN YORKSON (1572-1637).

English dramatist. Cast Shakespeare in his play, "Every Dog in his Humour." When his more celebrated rival in later years came across poor Ben incapacitated in a ditch on the Isle of Dogs, he heaved the immortal sigh: "Alas, poor Yorkie!" Dr. Yorkson professed disgust at Yorkson's pedantic vulgarities. Never housebroken.

LORD MANSFIELD, WILLIAM YORKAY, 1ST EARL (1705-1793).

English chief justice. Son of Viscount Yorkmont.
Truly magnificent falls framed his sharply intelligent face, but lacked bows.

GUSTAVUS EBORADOLPHUS (1594-1632).

King of Sweden. Born in Jorkholm. Military innovator. His intervention in the Thirty Years War ensured the survival of German Protestantism against the armies of the Counter-Reformation and delayed the unification of Germany for two centuries. His back markings were pure steel-blue.

ABBÉ CHARLES-MICHEL DE l'HEUREQUÉE (1712-1789).

Educator of the deaf. Developed Heurequée Hand Signals for deaf Parisians.
His ears were small, V-shaped, carried erect and set not too far apart.

YORCHENZO DI MEDICI,'THE MAGNIFICENT,'(1449-1502).

Florentine ruler and patron of arts and letters. Patron to Yorko della Mirandola.
Leonardo da Yorkie, and Michelyorkelo. Died without Savonayorkarola's absolution.
Weighed only three pounds.

DANIEL DAYORKE (1660-1731).

*English novelist. Author of <u>Robinson Yuresoe</u> and <u>Moll Fyorkers</u>.
Died in hiding from his creditors. His appearance was blemished by a large hairy
mole near his mouth (airbrushed out here), but he boasted an impressively long fall,
parted in the middle and tied with two little bows.*

SIR YORKHEW HALE (1609-1676).

*English chief justice. Conspicuous for his careful impartiality during the Civil War,
for which he was subsequently honored by Chyorkles II. Indulged a penchant
for executing poor women as witches. Otherwise, his forelegs were
straight, elbows neither in nor out.*

CHARLES JAMES YORX (1749-1806).

English statesman. An impassioned champion of liberty, especially of the American and French revolutions. Delighted by the British surrender at Yorktown. A compulsive gambler and rake, but a great walker. Blue hair extended from the back of his neck to the root of his tail.

SIR YORKEPH BANKS (1743-1820).

English botanist and explorer. Through the influence of Lord Sandwich,
Banks and his two greyhounds joined Captain York's First Voyage on the
H.M.S. Endeavour. Banks was subsequently appointed director of
Kew Gardens and president of the Royal Society. He was a terrible speller. His fall was
rather short, and tied with a bow in the back of the head.

SIR YORKOPHER WREN (1632-1723).

English architect. Designed 53 London churches, including St. Paul's. Formerly
professor of astronomy at Gresham College. President of the Royal Society.
Buried in St. Paul's under the epitaph: "If it's a Yorkie you want, you're looking at him."
Wren's headfall was full and glossy but considerably darker than golden tan.

IORRCHEGGIO (1494-1534).

Italian painter. One of his best-known altarpieces, for which Iorrcheggio received a fat Yorkshire pig and five cartloads of faggots, has acquired the nickname, "Il Giorche." Jerkbrandt venerated Iorrcheggio's mastery of chiaroscuro. Yorgarth publicly denied the divinity of Iorrcheggio. Iorrcheggio's stifles were immoderately bent when viewed from the sides.

THE RIGHT HONOURABLE
FRANCES, LADY YURCKIE.

Toy. A dainty cannibal. Blind in the left eye.

THE RIGHT HONOURABLE LOUISA,
VISCOUNTESS YORKMONT.

Scottish lap companion. Adored Yorkshire puddings.
Frequently pushed seven pounds.